Étienne de La Boétie
The Discourse of Voluntary Servitude

ERIS
gems

I COME NOW TO A POINT WHICH IS, IN my opinion, the mainspring and the secret of domination, the support and foundation of tyranny. Whoever thinks that halberds, sentries, the placing of the watch, serve to protect and shield tyrants is, in my judgment, completely mistaken. These are used, it seems to me, more for ceremony and a show of force than for any reliance placed in them. The archers forbid the entrance to the palace to the poorly dressed who have no weapons, not to the well armed who can carry out some plot. Certainly it is easy to say of the Roman emperors that fewer escaped from danger by the aid of their guards than were killed by their own archers. It is not the troops on horseback, it is not the companies afoot, it is not arms that defend the tyrant. This does not seem credible on first thought, but it is nevertheless true that there are only four or five who maintain the dictator, four or five who keep the country in bondage to him. Five or six have always had access to his ear, and have either gone to him of their own accord, or else have been summoned by him, to be accomplices in his cruelties, companions in his pleasures, panders to his lusts, and sharers in his plunders. These six manage their chief so successfully that he comes to be held accountable not only for his own misdeeds but even for theirs. The six have six hundred who profit under them, and with the six hundred they do what they have accomplished with their tyrant. The six hundred maintain under them six thousand, whom they promote in rank, upon whom they confer the government of provinces or the direction of finances, in order that they may serve as instruments of avarice and cruelty, executing orders at the proper time and working such havoc all around that they could not last except under the shadow of the six hundred, nor be exempt from law and punishment except through their influence.

The consequence of all this is fatal indeed. And whoever is pleased to unwind the skein will observe that not the six thousand but a hundred thousand, and even millions, cling to the tyrant by this cord to which they are tied. According to Homer, Jupiter boasts of being able to draw to himself all the gods when he pulls a chain. Such a scheme caused the increase in the senate under Julius, the formation of new ranks, the creation of offices; not really, if properly considered, to reform justice, but to provide new supporters of despotism. In short, when the point is reached, through big favors or little ones, that large profits or small are obtained under a tyrant, there are found almost as many people to whom tyranny seems advantageous as those to whom liberty would seem desirable. Doctors declare that if, when some part of the body has gangrene a disturbance arises in another spot, it immediately flows to the troubled part. Even so, whenever a ruler makes himself a dictator, all the wicked dregs of the nation—I do not mean the pack of petty thieves and earless ruffians who, in a republic, are unimportant in evil or good—but all those who are corrupted by burning ambition or extraordinary avarice, these gather round him and support him in order to have a share in the booty and to constitute themselves petty chiefs under the big tyrant. This is the practice among notorious robbers and famous pirates: some scour the country, others pursue voyagers; some lie in ambush, others keep a lookout; some commit murder, others robbery; and although there are among them differences in rank, some being only underlings while others are chieftains of gangs, yet is there not a single one among them who does not feel himself to be a sharer, if not of the main booty, at least in the pursuit of it. It is dependably related that Sicilian pirates gathered in such great numbers that it became necessary to send against them Pompey the Great, and that they drew into their alliance fine towns and great cities in whose harbors they took refuge on returning from their expeditions, paying handsomely for the haven given their stolen goods.

Thus the despot subdues his subjects, some of them by means of others, and thus is he protected by those from whom, if they were decent men, he would have to guard himself; just as, in order to split wood, one has to use a wedge of the wood itself. Such are his archers, his guards, his halberdiers; not that they themselves do not suffer occasionally at his hands, but this riff-raff, abandoned alike by God and man, can be led to endure evil if permitted to commit it, not against him who exploits them, but against those who like themselves submit, but are helpless. Nevertheless, observing those men who painfully serve the tyrant in order to win some profit from his tyranny and from the subjection of the populace, I am often overcome with amazement at their wickedness and sometimes by pity for their folly. For, in all honesty, can it be in any way except in folly that you approach a tyrant, withdrawing further from your liberty and, so to speak, embracing with both hands your servitude? Let such men lay aside briefly their ambition, or let them forget for a moment their avarice, and look at themselves as they really are. Then they will realize clearly that the townspeople, the peasants whom they trample under foot and treat worse than convicts or slaves, they will realize, I say, that these people, mistreated as they may be, are nevertheless, in comparison with themselves, better off and fairly free. The tiller of the soil and the artisan, no matter how enslaved, discharge their obligation when they do what they are told to do; but the dictator sees men about him wooing and begging his favor, and doing much more than he tells them to do. Such men must not only obey orders; they must anticipate his wishes; to satisfy him they must foresee his desires; they must wear themselves out, torment themselves, kill themselves with work in his interest, and accept his pleasure as their own, neglecting their preferences for his, distorting their character and corrupting their nature; they must pay heed to his words, to his intonation, to his gestures, and to his glance. Let them have no eye, nor foot, nor hand that is not alert to respond to his wishes or to seek out his thoughts.

Can that be called a happy life? Can it be called living? Is there anything more intolerable than that situation, I won't say for a man of mettle nor even for a man of high birth, but simply for a man of common sense or, to go even further, for anyone having the face of a man? What condition is more wretched than to live thus, with nothing to call one's own, receiving from someone else one's sustenance, one's power to act, one's body, one's very life?

Still men accept servility in order to acquire wealth; as if they could acquire anything of their own when they cannot even assert that they belong to themselves, or as if anyone could possess under a tyrant a single thing in his own name. Yet they act as if their wealth really belonged to them, and forget that it is they themselves who give the ruler the power to deprive everybody of everything, leaving nothing that anyone can identify as belonging to somebody. They notice that nothing makes men so subservient to a tyrant's cruelty as property; that the possession of wealth is the worst of crimes against him, punishable even by death; that he loves nothing quite so much as money and ruins only the rich, who come before him as before a butcher, offering themselves so stuffed and bulging that they make his mouth water. These favorites should not recall so much the memory of those who have won great wealth from tyrants as of those who, after they had for some time amassed it, have lost to him their property as well as their lives; they should consider not how many others have gained a fortune, but rather how few of them have kept it. Whether we examine ancient history or simply the times in which we live, we shall see clearly how great is the number of those who, having by shameful means won the ear of princes—who either profit from their villainies or take advantage of their naïveté—were in the end reduced to nothing by these very princes; and although at first such servitors were met by a ready willingness to promote their interests, they later found an equally obvious inconstancy which brought them to ruin. Certainly among so large a number of people who have at one time or another had some relationship with bad rulers, there have been few or practically none at all who have not felt applied to themselves the tyrant's animosity, which they had formerly stirred up against others. Most often, after becoming rich by despoiling others, under the favor of his protection, they find themselves at last enriching him with their own spoils.

Even men of character—if it sometimes happens that a tyrant likes such a man well enough to hold him in his good graces, because in him shine forth the virtue and integrity that inspire a certain reverence even in the most depraved—even men of character, I say, could not long avoid succumbing to the common malady and would early experience the effects of tyranny at their own expense. A Seneca, a Burrus, a Thrasea, this triumvirate of splendid men, will provide a sufficient reminder of such misfortune. Two of them were close to the tyrant by the fatal responsibility of holding in their hands the management of his affairs, and both were esteemed and beloved by him. One of them, moreover, had a peculiar claim upon his friendship, having instructed his master as a child. Yet these three by their cruel death give sufficient evidence of how little faith one can place in the friendship of an evil ruler. Indeed what friendship may be expected from one whose heart is bitter enough to hate even his own people, who do naught else but obey him? It is because he does not know how to love that he ultimately impoverishes his own spirit and destroys his own empire.

Now if one would argue that these men fell into disgrace because they wanted to act honorably, let him look around boldly at others close to that same tyrant, and he will see that those who came into his favor and maintained themselves by dishonorable means did not fare much better. Who has ever heard tell of a love more centered, of an affection more persistent, who has ever read of a man more desperately attached to a woman than Nero was to Poppaea? Yet she was later poisoned by his own hand. Agrippina his mother had killed her husband, Claudius, in order to exalt her son; to gratify him she had never hesitated at doing or bearing anything; and yet this very son, her offspring, her emperor, elevated by her hand, after failing her often, finally took her life. It is indeed true that no one denies she would have well deserved this punishment, if only it had come to her by some other hand than that of the son she had brought into the world. Who was ever more easily managed, more naive, or, to speak quite frankly, a greater simpleton, than Claudius the Emperor? Who was ever more wrapped up in his wife than he in Messalina, whom he delivered finally into the hands of the executioner? Stupidity in a tyrant always renders him incapable of benevolent action; but in some mysterious way by dint of acting cruelly even towards those who are his closest associates, he seems to manifest what little intelligence he may have.

Quite generally known is the striking phrase of that other tyrant who, gazing at the throat of his wife, a woman he dearly loved and without whom it seemed he could not live, caressed her with this charming comment: "This lovely throat would be cut at once if I but gave the order." That is why the majority of the dictators of former days were commonly slain by their closest favorites who, observing the nature of tyranny, could not be so confident of the whim of the tyrant as they were distrustful of his power. Thus was Domitian killed by Stephen, Commodus by one of his mistresses, Antoninus by Macrinus, and practically all the others in similar violent fashion. The fact is that the tyrant is never truly loved, nor does he love. Friendship is a sacred word, a holy thing; it is never developed except between persons of character, and never takes root except through mutual respect; it flourishes not so much by kindnesses as by sincerity. What makes one friend sure of another is the knowledge of his integrity: as guarantees he has his friend's fine nature, his honor, and his constancy. There can be no friendship where there is cruelty, where there is disloyalty, where there is injustice. And in places where the wicked gather there is conspiracy only, not companionship: these have no affection for one another; fear alone holds them together; they are not friends, they are merely accomplices.

Although it might not be impossible, yet it would be difficult to find true friendship in a tyrant; elevated above others and having no companions, he finds himself already beyond the pale of friendship, which receives its real sustenance from an equality that, to proceed without a limp, must have its two limbs equal. That is why there is honor among thieves (or so it is reported) in the sharing of the booty; they are peers and comrades; if they are not fond of one another they at least respect one another and do not seek to lessen their strength by squabbling. But the favorites of a tyrant can never feel entirely secure, and the less so because he has learned from them that he is all powerful and unlimited by any law or obligation. Thus it becomes his wont to consider his own will as reason enough, and to be master of all with never a compeer. Therefore it seems a pity that with so many examples at hand, with the danger always present, no one is anxious to act the wise man at the expense of the others, and that among so many persons fawning upon their ruler there is not a single one who has the wisdom and the boldness to say to him what, according to the fable, the fox said to the lion who feigned illness: "I should be glad to enter your lair to pay my respects; but I see many tracks of beasts that have gone toward you, yet not a single trace of any who have come back."

These wretches see the glint of the despot's treasures and are bedazzled by the radiance of his splendor. Drawn by this brilliance they come near, without realizing they are approaching a flame that cannot fail to scorch them. Similarly attracted, the indiscreet satyr of the old fables, on seeing the bright fire brought down by Prometheus, found it so beautiful that he went and kissed it, and was burned; so, as the Tuscan poet reminds us, the moth, intent upon desire, seeks the flame because it shines, and also experiences its other quality, the burning. Moreover, even admitting that favorites may at times escape from the hands of him they serve, they are never safe from the ruler who comes after him. If he is good, they must render an account of their past and recognize at last that justice exists; if he is bad and resembles their late master, he will certainly have his own favorites, who are not usually satisfied to occupy in their turn merely the posts of their predecessors, but will more often insist on their wealth and their lives. Can anyone be found, then, who under such perilous circumstances and with so little security will still be ambitious to fill such an ill-fated position and serve, despite such perils, so dangerous a master? Good God, what suffering, what martrydom all this involves! To be occupied night and day in planning to please one person, and yet to fear him more than anyone else in the world; to be always on the watch, ears open, wondering whence the blow will come; to search out conspiracy, to be on guard against snares, to scan the faces of companions for signs of treachery, to smile at everybody and be mortally afraid of all, to be sure of nobody, either as an open enemy or as a reliable friend; showing always a gay countenance despite an apprehensive heart, unable to be joyous yet not daring to be sad!

However, there is satisfaction in examining what they get out of all this torment, what advantage they derive from all the trouble of their wretched existence. Actually the people never blame the tyrant for the evils they suffer, but they do place responsibility on those who influence him; peoples, nations, all compete with one another, even the peasants, even the tillers of the soil, in mentioning the names of the favorites, in analyzing their vices, and heaping upon them a thousand insults, a thousand obscenities, a thousand maledictions. All their prayers, all their vows are directed against these persons; they hold them accountable for all their misfortunes, their pestilences, their famines; and if at times they show them outward respect, at those very moments they are fuming in their hearts and hold them in greater horror than wild beasts. This is the glory and honor heaped upon influential favorites for their services by people who, if they could tear apart their living bodies, would still clamor for more, only half satiated by the agony they might behold. For even when the favorites are dead those who live after are never too lazy to blacken the names of these man-eaters with the ink of a thousand pens, tear their reputations into bits in a thousand books, and drag, so to speak, their bones past posterity, forever punishing them after their death for their wicked lives.

Let us therefore learn while there is yet time, let us learn to do good. Let us raise our eyes to Heaven for the sake of our honor, for the very love of virtue, or, to speak wisely, for the love and praise of God Almighty, who is the infallible witness of our deeds and the just judge of our faults. As for me, I truly believe I am right, since there is nothing so contrary to a generous and loving God as dictatorship—I believe He has reserved, in a separate spot in Hell, some very special punishment for tyrants and their accomplices.

ERIS

265 Riverside Dr.
New York, NY 10025

ISBN 978-1-967751-11-2

This third part of Étienne de La Boétie's *The Discourse of Voluntary Servitude* originally published (clandestinely) in 1577.

eris.press